THE PHOTOGRAPHER'S ORGANIZER

BY

MICHAL HERON

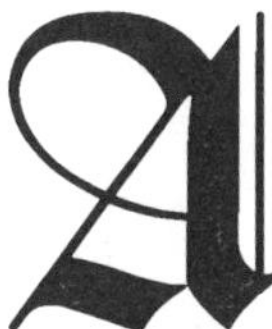

ALLWORTH PRESS, NEW YORK

Published by **Allworth Press**, an imprint of
Allworth Communications, Inc., 10 East 23rd Street, New York, NY 10010.

Distributor to the trade in the United States:
Consortium Book Sales & Distribution, Inc.
287 East Sixth Street, Suite 365
Saint Paul, MN 55101.

Distributor to photographic supply outlets:
Amphoto Books
1515 Broadway
New York, NY 10036

Book design by Douglas Design Associates, New York, NY.

ISBN: 1-880559-02-1

TABLE OF CONTENTS

It's easy to get bogged down by the organizational aspects of your photography. Creative people often find it especially hard to cope with dry subjects like insurance and taxes, or tracking the details of a photo shoot. The necessary but often tedious paperwork, if not well managed, can drain time and energy way out of proportion with the actual time needed for the work. The dread takes more time than the task. Procrastination sets in and you're sunk.

The forms in this book were developed for my business in an effort to fight my way out of that quandry. I determined not to let the details strangle me.

So, there is no need to balk at the mention of taxes, insurance or promotion mailer cost estimates. Use these forms to help make a safety net for the valuable fragments of information you collect every day. Have that information accessible, in an organized, orderly structure when you need it,

If your computer has the capability, these forms can be scanned into the computer for adaptation to your own business needs.

The discussion of the forms follows the sequence of the forms as they appear in the book.

Photo Project Record

The Photo Project Record is a quick reference tool. It can be used as a guide to all your projects, providing information at a glance about all photographs whether shot on assignment, self-assigned as stock, travel shoots, personal work, experimentation or even vacation shooting.

It serves as a chronological log of your shooting, helping you identify a specific shoot easily, even years later, with just a quick look. No matter how busy you are, this form is easy to keep up to date. It is most helpful when used as a companion to the Photo Job Form.

Photo Job Form

This is the in-depth form which backs up the Photo Project Record. The Photo Job form can provide a detailed profile on each shoot by having a place for all information relating to the paperwork of the shoot.

You can keep on top of current activities like sending complimentary prints and thank you letters to models or you can track down information from the past. If you are seting up another trip to Mesa Verde and want to find the Park Ranger who helped you three years ago during a shoot, you'll find the name on your Photo Job Form.

Casting Form/Model File

This form serves a dual purpose. You can use it to make auditioning large groups of models much easier since it helps reduce the chaos of a "go-see". As they arrive, have the models fill in the pertinent information. Then, as you interview each person, make your own notes on the sheet. (I write such comments as "sparkly eyes", "nice dimples", or "Chubby but cute". I'll also note if they read as a particular type or role, for example, "energetic elderly" or "Hispanic professional".)

If you shoot a polaroid, attach it along with any head shot the model brings. This makes a large audition move quickly and smoothly. Of course, you'll use the form to gather information from any individual models that you meet.

After it's filled in, the form serves as a permanent record in your model file.

Photo File Categories

Once you've acquired a reasonable number of professional photographs and become serious about selling them, it's necessary to set up some form of filing system (no matter how simple). Otherwise, you'll never find what you want when it's needed. Start as early in your career as possible before the task becomes daunting.

There are two basic approaches to filing photographs: chronologically by shoot or by subject category. Your decision on filing method will be based on the way you shoot and the way you market your photography.

If you market stories to magazines, then you might prefer to stay with a chronological system and keep each story or shoot intact. But if your requests come in by topic or concept, then you will find a category file more useful.

If you choose to file by topic, use the basic list of photo categories and adapt them to your specialty. For example, if you shoot wildlife, you will want to expand the nature, animals, geology, environment, and pollution sections. If you travel a lot, then you'll add categories for different countries, cities, regions — with further breakdowns for crafts, customs, holidays, and language signs in each country. If people are your specialty, you will add breakdowns for infants, babies, children, teens, adults, couples, family and seniors, divided further by ethnic background or activity.

Categories are presented here alphabetically. However, if you file by topic, I suggest you group them by subject area. For example, agriculture, gardens, horticulture and their subdivisions would be under the main section Agriculture. This fine-tuning depends entirely on the type of pictures you take. Use the form provided as a worksheet for developing your file headings. The most important thing is to start and methodically continue with your system.

Assistant File Sheet and Stylist File Sheet

These forms keep track of people you have worked with or those whose names you've gotten from colleagues. When you suddenly need someone on short notice for a job, it's a great help to have all of this information organized and accessible.

Photo Suppliers

Having these listings in one place is especially handy if you are getting competitive quotations on equipment or services. Make extra copies for dealing with additional suppliers.

Client Sheet

Getting in the door with a photo buyer, whether for stock or assignment, takes persistence and organization. Usually, it requires repeated phone calls before you get an appointment to show your portfolio. Keeping track of these calls is much easier with this form.

Be sure to note what was said on each call when you actually speak to a client (don't bother recording the attempts that didn't get through). Develop your own note-taking code. A successful advertising photographer friend, who spends much of his life calling clients, uses "sb" to indicate "spoke briefly" with the date and a note on when the client said he should call back ("cb").

A cardinal rule is to find out if the client is too busy to talk. Sometimes you can tell by the harried tone of voice. Your remark: "Is this a bad time? When would it be better to call?" will win you appreciation, especially if you get off the phone very fast. Your note might read: "sb/cb week 6/4."

On longer conversations, make notes on any business information gleaned, such as "we're slow now but should be gearing up in September." Also, it doesn't hurt to show some personal interest. If you have kept notes of casual remarks made by the client: "I'm looking for a chemistry set for my son's birthday" or "We're about to leave on a skiing trip," then on a subsequent call you can ask how the boy liked his present or if the skiing was good. You'll be met with pleasant surprise. If you regularly see lots of clients, make extra copies for additional follow-up calls and for each person within the company that you deal with — Art Director, Art Buyer, and Photo Researcher.

Promotion Planner

Promotion materials keep your name and your work in front of the photo buyer when you're not there in person. It's important to evaluate each card or brochure you have printed in terms of the value for the cost.

Use this form to prepare a profile history of each piece of promotional mailing you have created. Based on the response you get from clients, you can assess the value in cost for each. It also provides a tidy way to keep suppliers' names accessible.

You can also use the form to gather comparative price quotations in the space provided. Then after you've made the decision and printed the materials, complete the history of each mailer for future reference and evaluation.

Travel Information

This form has the obvious benefit of keeping your primary travel sources easily grouped together. Copy extra sheets to add numbers or to segregate by country.

Travel Contacts

This form can be copied onto paper or card stock depending on your filing preference.

Generally, you will use an entire sheet for each country or, in some cases, for a city or region. If you have traveled extensively in Spain, you might make separate files for Madrid, Barcelona, Nerja and Alcudia. Or you might simply sort your contacts by region, such as Napa Valley, or the Algarve.

It's handy to fill out this form before leaving on a trip if you have some suggested names from friends or colleagues to look up or some people whom you've already contacted by phone. Take along a photocopy in your travel kit. Then, when you return, fill in any new contacts you've made on the original forms which stay in your file. Enter the date when you met the person.

This invaluable information originates on random note paper, the back of someone's business card or on cocktail napkins. Transferring it to this form means it will be just where you want it next time you need it.

The comment section can be used for a description of a special knowledge (such as: "knows museums", or "has good entreé to wildlife refuges") or special skills (such as: "has diving license", or "owns a 4-wheel drive vehicle").

After you return home you can use the form to check off whether thank you letters or complimentary prints were sent.

Budget

For many people the thought of creating a budget is about as appealing as a trip to the dentist. For others it is the sheer effort that deters them. This form makes it easy. If you simply enter the expenses on the form each time you pay a bill, within a short time you'll have the figures to help plan your finances.

Business expenses fall into two distinct categories. The first are usually called fixed costs — those that recur and remain relatively constant. These are expenses that you have to pay whether or not you are doing any photography work at all. It's your cost to open the door and turn the lights on. These costs can be predicted and planned for in your budget.

Variable costs are those that change according to how much shooting you are doing. Or they are discretionary, such as how much you will spend on promotion or new equipment. In budget terms they can only be estimated.

Why make a budget? Whether you run a large business with employees or a part-time operation out of your own home, controlling your finances is essential and makes it easier to maintain the creative end of your business.

There are four reasons for keeping track of costs:

- It helps you to prepare for taxes.

- It helps control cash flow by anticipating what payments are due and when.

- It enables you to plan capital expenditures, such as the purchase of new equipment.

- It allows you to price your work more accurately and to learn if you are making a profit or losing money from your photography.

Financial Reference Sheet

In addition to your own use, this form is especially important to leave with your family when you're away. In case of illness or emergency, it's a great help to have this and your legal information readily at hand for those who might need it.

Business Equipment Insurance List

Listing all your equipment, as you buy it will make handling insurance much easier. It also aids your accountant in figuring the amount of depreciation to list as an expense on your tax return.

Tax Calendar

Use this handy checklist to make sure you've met all your tax obligations.

Tax Worksheet

This form helps you gather information easily and present it in a way that's useful for your accountant or for yourself if you do your own taxes.

The categories are organized to correspond (roughly) to the IRS form Schedule C, Profit and Loss from a Business.   The IRS plays around with their forms, so the order can change slightly from year to year, but the basic categories of information stay the same.

The worksheet information is valuable if you ever have to go back to figure out how you arrived at certain figures.

Estimated Tax Worksheet

Note the payment of estimated taxes in the section provided. When you need it at tax time, there's no doubt about what you've paid. (And you don't have to fumble through the check book.) You can keep two year's estimated taxes on one form for easier reference.

Legal Reference Sheet

This serves the obvious purpose of having all your information together. It should be filed in your office and also with your executor or in your safe deposit box, wherever you have important papers.

Estate Organizer

Once you have made a will setting out your wishes as to the disposition of your property to your beneficiaries, you can take other steps to help make the settling of your estate as trouble free as possible for your heirs.

By preparing careful, detailed suggestions about the handling of your photographs and also giving information about your files, you can dramatically improve the probate process. However, if you leave matters to chance, with your records and photographic files in disarray, you may cause an expensive and nightmarish crisis for your heirs.

Photographs that have earned money for you, or have the potential to produce income during your life and over the life of the copyright (your life plus fifty years), can be significant assets of your estate after your death. These assets will be subject to appraisal and to estate taxes on the federal and in many cases the state level. (In some instances the state taxing authority will accept the determination of the IRS.)

How does the IRS know you have professional photographs to appraise? If you've ever gotten a 1099 form for income from photography, then you may be subject to appraisal.

The first step in the process of appraising your photographic file is to determine a method of valuation. Taxes are assessed by the IRS based on the value resulting from the appraisal.

If the photographic portion of your estate is assessed by the IRS at an inaccurately high valuation, this could cause a financial crisis in terms of estate taxes. This might happen, for example, if every one of your out-of-focus rejects or casual snapshots were erroneously valued as professional, income-producing photographs.

For that reason it is critical that you make distinctions about which of your photographs actually have income producing value and which do not. Also, a professional look to your files will lend credibility when your executor is dealing with the IRS.

Here's what you should do, starting now and continuing during your lifetime:

❑ Clean out your files periodically. Throw away anything not of commercial, artistic or sentimental value. For this discussion, commercial is defined as any photograph with income-producing potential whether for the advertising, editorial or any other market.

❑ Separate, categorize and clearly label any pictures that you choose not to throw out but which don't have current or future commercial value. Keeping the noncommercial material physically separate is critical to the success of this estate housekeeping.

❑ Make a clear outline of your files with a list of the categories and the labeling system you've used to differentiate the commercially valuable photographs from the rest. Make sure to mention the locations of these separate categories of photographs. For example: My snapshot file is in the brown cabinet in the back closet of the studio.

❑ Prepare a memo to your executor which fully explains your breakdown of categories of photographs. Keep the memo with your will. The Estate Organizer form gives an approach to this memo and some categories which you can adapt to your own business.

If you have special collections that would be of interest to a museum or research institution — such as, coverage of Native Americans or rare species of marine life — you may use the Estate Organizer to mention that the heirs might wish to donate this collection to an institution in order to secure tax savings. You may have already made such a decision to donate, and stipulated it in your will. If not, mentioning it in a memo is merely a way of presenting alternatives to your heirs without tying their hands.

Also, make clear to your executor that the photographs in your stock file — which you have been selling through your own photo business — must be organized and reevaluated if they are to continue to produce income. Unless you have a partner who will continue to maintain your files, this material will more than likely need to be edited and presented to your stock agency. The expense of this edit may be deducted from the estate.

Appraisal valuation for photographs on file with a stock agency is often computed on an average of the past five year's earnings. You may suggest that this method of appraisal be used. Make clear where information on your stock income can be found in the sales reports from your agency.

Consider having a special photographic consultant to your executor, a person knowledgeable in the photography business, and list that name along with your stock agency information.

Using the Estate Organizer will prompt you to answer questions about the handling of your photographs that you may not have considered — questions which could puzzle and confuse your heirs if left unanswered.

The information in this book is not intended as an estate plan. These suggestions on how to organize your photographic material as well as use of a photographic advisor should be discussed with your lawyer.

For more helpful information on this subject, consult the excellent discussion in *Legal Guide for Visual Artist* by Tad Crawford, published by Allworth Press and the *ASMP Stock Photography Handbook* which has a fine chapter on estate planning.

A little effort now, when the issue of your estate seems a distant concern, can be of enormous benefit to your heirs later on.

PHOTO PROJECT RECORD

JOB #	SHOT FOR		CLIENT	PROJECT	DATE OF SHOOT	DATE RELEASED TO STOCK
	ASSIGN	STOCK				

PHOTO JOB FORM

Job # _________________   ❏ Assignment   ❏ Stock   Photos filed in category _________________

Photo shoot title ____

Description ____

Rights granted/restriction ____

Client ____

Address ____

____

Phone _____________________   Fax _____________________

Contact ____

	<u>Action Date</u>	<u>Completed on</u>
Shoot date		
Film edited		
Model/prop release filed with polaroid		
Selects captioned/model Release #		
Sent to client (via __________)		
Fee & Expenses billed		
Photos returned from client		
Edit photos for stock agency		
Numbered with file numbers		
Time restriction up		
Sent to photo agency		
Model slides picked		
Labels (model address)		
Slides to prints		
Pick-up prints		
Thank you letter/Prints to models		
Tearsheets requested from client		

Location of shoot _______________________________________

Address _______________________________________

Contact person _______________________________________

MODELS   Name _______________________________________

Address _______________________________________

____

Phone _____________________   Model Release # _____________

(Attach Sheet for additional models)

CASTING FORM / MODEL FILE

Date ______________________   ❑ Adult   ❑ Child

Model's name ____

Address ____

____

Phone (home) ________________________   Phone (work) ______________________

Fax ________________________________

Clothing sizes

Age range ____________________   Shirt __________________

Birth date ____________________   Pants __________________

Hair color ____________________   Dress __________________

Eye color ____________________   Waist __________________

Height ____________________   Hat __________________

Weight ____________________   Glove __________________

Parent's name _______________________________________ (If applicable)

Child's grade/school ____

Teacher ____

Special abilities _________________________________

____

____

____

____

____

Attach Polaroid

Head sheet attached   ❑ Yes   ❑ No

❏ Abstracts	❏ Culture	❏ Government	❏ Military	❏ Seasons
❏ Agriculture	❏ Drug/Abuse	❏ Health	❏ Nature	❏ Special Effects
❏ Alchohol/Abuse	❏ Education	❏ Holidays/festivals	❏ Occupations	❏ Sports
❏ Animals	❏ Environment	❏ Horticulture	❏ People	❏ Still Life
❏ Architecture	❏ Executives	❏ Housing	❏ Pollution	❏ Stores
❏ Business	❏ Food	❏ Industry	❏ Religion	❏ Symbols
❏ Communications	❏ Flowers	❏ Landscape	❏ Research	❏ Travel
❏ Concepts	❏ Gardens	❏ Leisure	❏ Restaurants	❏ Transportation
❏ Consumers	❏ Geography	❏ Medicine	❏ Scenics	❏ Urban
❏ Corporate	❏ Geology	❏ Mood/emotion	❏ Science	❏ Weather

Select from the list above the categories that best represent your collection. Enter each category on the top line of one of the columns below, then make subcategories beneath each heading to develop your complete file system.

ASSISTANT FILE SHEET

Date _______________________   **Fee:**   Day $__________

                                                                 Hourly $__________

Name ____   Soc. Sec. # ___________

Address ____

____

Phone ___________________________   Fax ___________________________

Ans. Service ___________________   Beeper___________________________

Referred by ____

Expertise in:

    Camera formats ____

    Strobes ____

    Darkroom: ❏ BW processing   ❏ BW printing   ❏ Color printing

    Set building ____

    Prop building ____

    Carpentry ____

Used on project _______________________________   Date _______________

Used on project _______________________________   Date _______________

Used on project _______________________________   Date _______________

Evaluation:

    Cameras ____

    Strobe ____

    General ability____

    Attitude ____

    Client rapport ____

Comments ____

____

____

____

STYLIST FILE SHEET

Date _______________________   **Fee:**   Day $ __________

                                         Hourly $ __________

                               Per picture $ __________

Name ____________________________________   Soc. Sec. # __________

Address ____

____

Phone _____________________   Fax _____________________

Ans. service _____________________   Beeper_____________________

Referred by ____

Expertise in:

    Location search ____

    Casting/model search _______________________________________

    Make-up ____

    Hair ____

    Prop buying ____

    Prop making ____

    Food styling ____

Used on project _______________________________   Date __________

Used on project _______________________________   Date __________

Used on project _______________________________   Date __________

Evaluation:

    Skills ____

    Attitude ____

    Client rapport ____

Comments ____

____

____

Camera Dealer (#1) ____

    Contact ________________________________ Phone ________________

    Address ________________________________ Fax ________________

____

Camera Dealer (#2) ____

    Contact ________________________________ Phone ________________

    Address ________________________________ Fax ________________

____

BW Lab ____

    Contact ________________________________ Phone ________________

    Address ________________________________ Fax ________________

____

Color Lab ____

    Contact ________________________________ Phone ________________

    Address ________________________________ Fax ________________

____

Camera Repair Service ____

    Contact ________________________________ Phone ________________

    Address ________________________________ Fax ________________

____

Lighting Supplier ____

    Contact ________________________________ Phone ________________

    Address ________________________________ Fax ________________

____

Filing/Archival Supplies ____

    Contact ________________________________ Phone ________________

    Address ________________________________ Fax ________________

____

Manufacturer's Tech Rep (Kodak Film) ____

    Contact ____   Phone ____________________

    Address ____   Fax ______________________

    ____

Manufacturer's Tech Rep (Fuji Film) ____

    Contact ____   Phone ____________________

    Address ____   Fax ______________________

    ____

Manufacturer's Tech Rep (Cameras) ____

    Contact ____   Phone ____________________

    Address ____   Fax ______________________

    ____

Manufacturer's Tech Rep (Cameras) ____

    Contact ____   Phone ____________________

    Address ____   Fax ______________________

    ____

Computer Supplies ____

    Contact ____   Phone ____________________

    Address ____   Fax ______________________

    ____

Software Suppliers

    Product ____________________________   Product ____________________________

    Company ____________________________   Company ____________________________

    Phone ____________________________   Phone ____________________________

    Tech. Support ____________________________   Tech. Support ____________________________

    Product ____________________________   Product ____________________________

    Company ____________________________   Company ____________________________

    Phone ____________________________   Phone ____________________________

    Tech. Support ____________________________   Tech. Support ____________________________

❑ Advertising Agency   ❑ Editorial/Magazine
❑ Corporate Advertising Dept.   ❑ Editorial/Book Publisher
❑ Corporate Communications   ❑ Public Relations Firm
❑ Design Firm   ❑ Other ___________________________

Company name _______________________________   Phone _______________

Address _______________________________   Fax _______________

____

Contact Name:

Art Director _______________________________   Ext. _______________

Art Buyer _______________________________   Ext. _______________

Designer _______________________________   Ext. _______________

Photo Editor _______________________________   Ext. _______________

Photo Researcher _______________________________   Ext. _______________

Contact for: ❑ Assignment   ❑ Stock

Called _______________________________ for appointment   Date _______________
    (name)

Comments _______________________________

1st Follow up call _______________________________ for appointment   Date _______________
    (name)

Comments _______________________________

2nd Follow up call _______________________________ for appointment   Date _______________
    (name)

Comments _______________________________

Appointment with _______________________________   Date _______________

Portfolio   ❑ Shown   ❑ Dropped off   Date _______________

Description of Photographs shown _______________________________

Promo pieces left   ❑ Yes   ❑ No   Description _______________________________

Client comments _______________________________

____

____

Call back made   ❑ Yes   ❑ No   Date _______________

Assignment resulting   ❑ Yes   ❑ No   Date _______________

Notes _______________________________

____

Description of Promotion Piece:

❏ Card ❏ Brochure ❏ Poster ❏ Other_______________

Printing Specifications:

Quantity ____________ Size ____________ ❏ 4 color process ❏ 2 PMS colors ❏ Duotone ❏ 1 color

Paper/stock ____ weight ________________

Finish: ❏ Uncoated ❏ Gloss coated ❏ Matte or Dull coated ❏ Varnished

Inks (Spot PMS or Duotone colors) ____

Special instructions ____

____

____

Photographs used ____

____

____

Graphic Designer

Firm _________________________________

Contact _______________________________

Address _______________________________

____

Phone ______________ Fax ______________

Separator

Firm _________________________________

Contact _______________________________

Address _______________________________

____

Phone ______________ Fax ______________

Printer

Firm _________________________________

Contact _______________________________

Address _______________________________

____

Phone ______________ Fax ______________

Mailing House

Firm _________________________________

Contact _______________________________

Address _______________________________

____

Phone ______________ Fax ______________

COSTS	Estimated	Estimated	Estimated	Actual
Photographic prep costs	__________	__________	__________	__________
Designer fee	__________	__________	__________	__________
Separation costs	__________	__________	__________	__________
Printing costs	__________	__________	__________	__________
Mailing/Handling	__________	__________	__________	__________
Postage	__________	__________	__________	__________
Misc.	__________	__________	__________	__________
Other ____________	__________	__________	__________	__________
Total Cost	__________	__________	__________	__________

Total cost per thousand $ ____________   Total cost per piece $ __________

Mailed to /List used ____

Travel Agency ____

Agent ____

Address ____

____

Phone _____________________________ Fax _____________________________

Passport Office (Local) ____

Address ____

____

Phone _____________________________

Passport Office	Passport/Visa Expediting Service
1425 K Street NW	Passport Services Inc.
Washington, DC 20524	10 Rockefeller Plaza, NY NY 10020
No Phone Listed	Phone: (212) 586-8880

Airlines _______________________________ Phone (local) _____________________

(800) _____________________

Airlines _______________________________ Phone (local) _____________________

(800) _____________________

Airlines _______________________________ Phone (local) _____________________

(800) _____________________

Train (Amtrack) _______________________________ Phone (local) _____________________

(800) _____________________

Train (other) _______________________________ Phone (local) _____________________

(800) _____________________

Hotel/Motel _______________________________ Phone (local) _____________________

(800) _____________________

Hotel/Motel _______________________________ Phone (local) _____________________

(800) _____________________

Hotel/Motel _______________________________ Phone (local) _____________________

(800) _____________________

Country	Visa	Innoculations	Other Requirements

TRAVEL CONTACTS

Date _____________________   Country/Region _____________________

Name ____

Affiliation _______________________________________

Address ____

____

Phone _____________________   Fax _____________________

Languages _________________   Referred by _____________________

Comments ____

____

____

Date _____________________   Country/Region _____________________

Name ____

Affiliation _______________________________________

Address ____

____

Phone _____________________   Fax _____________________

Languages _________________   Referred by _____________________

Comments ____

____

____

Date _____________________   Country/Region _____________________

Name ____

Affiliation _______________________________________

Address ____

____

Phone _____________________   Fax _____________________

Languages _________________   Referred by _____________________

Comments ____

____

____

FIXED COSTS	MONTHLY	QUARTERLY	YEARLY
Premises:			
Rent (studio/office)			
Rent (___% of home office)			
Mortgage (studio/office)			
Utilities:			
Telephone			
Electric			
Heat			
Insurance:			
Premiums			
Vehicle 1:			
Payment			
Mileage ___% business			
Vehicle 2:			
Payment			
Mileage ___% business			
Equipment - Photographic:			
Purchase/depreciation			
Rental			
Equipment - Business:			
Computer___________			
Purchase/depreciation			
Rental			
Copy machine___________			
Purchase/depreciation			
Rental			
Other___________			
Purchase/depreciation			
Rental			
Furnishings/fixtures:			
Purchase/depreciation			
Rental			
Taxes:			
Property Taxes			
Studio/Office			
___% of home space			
Employees:			
Salary (yourself)			
Salary (others)			
Payroll taxes			
Employee Benefits			
Misc. ___________			
TOTAL OF FIXED COSTS			

VARIABLE COSTS (estimated)	MONTHLY	QUARTERLY	YEARLY
Production Costs:			
Film			
Processing			
Model fees			
Props			
Permits			
Assistant's fees (freelance)			
Travel:			
Hotel			
Meals			
Air fare			
Car rental			
Transportation (other)			
Transportation (local)			
Studio/Office:			
Postage			
Office supplies			
Messenger/shipping			
Office help (temp)			
Repairs:			
Studio			
Photographic equipment			
Business equipment			
Promotion/advertising			
Mailing costs			
Periodical subscriptions/books			
Dues to professional associations			
Continuing education			
Other _______________			
Fees:			
Legal fees			
Accounting fees			
Bank costs			
Taxes:			
Federal			
State			
City			
Retirement:			
Pension plan			
Keogh contribution			
IRA contribution			
Misc. _______________			
Total of Variable Costs			
Total of Fixed Costs			
TOTAL BUDGET COSTS			

FINANCIAL REFERENCE SHEET

Accountant

Firm ___________________________   Phone (W)___________________

Contact ___________________________   Fax ___________________

Address ___________________________   Phone (H)___________________

___________________________   Fax ___________________

Mortgage #___________________

Bank ___________________________   Phone ___________________

Officer ___________________________   Ext. ___________________

Address ___________________________   Fax ___________________

____

Investment Account #___________________

Institution ___________________________   Phone ___________________

Broker ___________________________   Ext. ___________________

Address ___________________________   Fax ___________________

____

Keogh Retirement Account #___________________

Institution ___________________________   Phone ___________________

Officer ___________________________   Ext. ___________________

Address ___________________________   Fax ___________________

____

IRA Retirement Account #___________________

Institution ___________________________   Phone ___________________

Officer ___________________________   Ext. ___________________

Address ___________________________   Fax ___________________

____

Mutual Fund Account #___________________

Institution ___________________________   Phone ___________________

Officer ___________________________   Ext. ___________________

Address ___________________________   Fax ___________________

____

FINANCIAL REFERENCE SHEET

Business Checking Account #___________________________

    Bank ______________________________________   Phone ___________________

    Officer ____________________________________   Ext. _____________________

    Address ___________________________________   Fax _____________________

    ____

Personal Checking Account #___________________________

    Bank ______________________________________   Phone ___________________

    Officer ____________________________________   Ext. _____________________

    Address ___________________________________   Fax _____________________

    ____

Money Market Account #___________________________

    Bank ______________________________________   Phone ___________________

    Officer ____________________________________   Ext. _____________________

    Address ___________________________________   Fax _____________________

    ____

Savings Account #___________________________

    Bank ______________________________________   Phone ___________________

    Officer ____________________________________   Ext. _____________________

    Address ___________________________________   Fax _____________________

    ____

Credit Card Information

Credit card name __________________	Credit card name __________________
Credit card # __________________	Credit card # __________________
Exp. date _________ Credit limit $________	Exp. date _________ Credit limit $________
Bank issued __________________	Bank issued __________________
Emergency phone # __________________	Emergency phone # __________________
Credit card name __________________	Credit card name __________________
Credit card # __________________	Credit card # __________________
Exp. date _________ Credit limit $________	Exp. date _________ Credit limit $________
Bank issued __________________	Bank issued __________________
Emergency phone # __________________	Emergency phone # __________________

Credit Card Protection Service Name ___________________________   Phone___________________

BUSINESS EQUIPMENT INSURANCE LIST

DESCRIPTION	MANUFACTURER	SERIAL NUMBER	DATE OF PURCHASE	PURCHASE PRICE	LIFE OF EQUIP.
Camera Bodies & lenses					
Strobe & lighting					
Miscellaneous Accessories					
Office Equipment					
Computer					
Copy machine					
Fax machine					
Other					

- ❏ December — Do your year end tax planning.

- ❏ December 31 — If necessary, set up a Keogh Plan before year end.

- ❏ January 15 — File your fourth and final estimated tax payment for prior year.

- ❏ January 31 — If you have not filed your final estimated tax payment for prior year, file your prior year's income tax return and avoid an estimated tax penalty.

- ❏ January 31 — File a 1099–MISC (with its cover sheet, Form 1096) for each independent contractor whom you paid more than $600 during prior year.

- ❏ March 15 — Filing date for corporate returns.

- ❏ April 15 — File your income tax for prior year and pay any tax due.

- ❏ April 15 — Make your IRA contribution.

- ❏ April 15 — Your Keogh or SEP contribution must be made prior to filing your tax return. If you are extending the time to file your return, the time to make your Keogh or SEP contribution is also extended.

- ❏ April 15 — File Form 4868 to receive an automatic four month extension. You must pay the amount of tax that you estimate will be due.

- ❏ April 15 — Pay the first installment for your current year's estimated taxes. This may be covered by applying an overpayment of your prior year's taxes toward your current year's estimated tax.

- ❏ April 15 — File your gift tax return if you made taxable gifts during the prior year.

- ❏ June 15 — Pay the second installment for your current year's estimated taxes.

- ❏ July 31 — File Form 5500 for your Keogh plan whether or not you made a contribution during the prior year. If your plan covers only you or you and your spouse who wholly own your business, you can file Form 5500EZ. No form at all need be filed if you qualify to use Form 5500EZ and the total assets of your plan are $100,000 or less at the end of the plan year.

- ❏ August 15 — If you received a four-month extension to file your income taxes, either file and pay now or apply for an additional two-month extension using Form 2688.

- ❏ September 15 — Pay the third installment for your current year's estimated taxes.

- ❏ October 15 — If you received a four-month and a two-month extension, file your income tax form for the prior year and pay taxes, interest, and penalties due.

- ❏ December — Do your year end tax planning.

- ❏ December 31 — If necessary, set up a Keogh Plan before year end.

- ❏ January 15 — Pay the final estimated tax installment for the prior tax year.

PHOTOGRAPHY BUSINESS INCOME

Tax Year_________________   Page 1 of __________

Name ____   Soc.Sec.# _____________________

Business Name _____________________________________   Fed. ID# _____________________

Address ____   Phone _______________________

____

Total 1099's	$ ___________________
Photography income (no 1099)	$ ___________________
Photo Lecture/Seminar fees	$ ___________________
Royalty Payments	$ ___________________
Interest from business savings account	$ ___________________
Total Photography Income	___________________

PHOTOGRAPHY BUSINESS EXPENSES

Item	Transaction made by				Total Expense
	Check	**Credit Card**	**Cash**	**Cash diary entry**	
Advertising					
Bad debts					
Car/truck mileage __________					
miles @ __________					
Or vehicle expenses					
Depreciation					
Employee benefits					
Professional dues & publication					
Insurance (business/camera)					
Health insurance					
Mortgage interest					
Studio/office					
Legal/professional fees					
Office expense					
Pension plan					
Rent/lease equipment					
Total expenses Page One					

PHOTOGRAPHY BUSINESS EXPENSES (Continued)

Item	Transaction made by				Total Expense
	Check	**Credit Card**	**Cash**	**Cash diary entry**	
Rent/lease business property					
Repairs/photo equipment					
Repairs/other					
Supplies					
Postage					
Stationery					
Office supplies misc.					
Taxes					
Travel					
Meals & Entertainment					
Utilities					
Telephone					
Transportation local					
Messengers/shipping					
Salaries					
Freelancers (Check box if 1099 needed)					
❏ Name_______________					
❏ Name_______________					
❏ Name_______________					
❏ Name_______________					
Total freelance fees					
Model fees					
Office temporary					
Materials - film					
Film processing					
Other _______________					
Other _______________					

Total from Page One _______________

TOTAL EXPENSES

Estimated Tax

Tax Year_______________

Name ____   Soc.Sec. # _____________________

	IRS		State		City		Total Due
	Amt Due	**Amt Paid** **Ck # Date**	**Amt Due**	**Amt Paid** **Ck # Date**	**Amt Due**	**Amt Paid** **Ck # Date**	
4/15							
6/15							
9/15							
1/15/__							
Total Year							

Estimated Tax

Tax Year_______________

Name ____   Soc.Sec. # _____________________

	IRS		State		City		Total Due
	Amt Due	**Amt Paid** **Ck # Date**	**Amt Due**	**Amt Paid** **Ck # Date**	**Amt Due**	**Amt Paid** **Ck # Date**	
4/15							
6/15							
9/15							
1/15/__							
Total Year							

LEGAL INFORMATION REFERENCE SHEET

Lawyer — Photographic Business

Name ____

Firm ____ Phone ______________________

Address _____________________________________ Fax ________________________

____

Lawyer — Family matters

Name ____

Firm ____ Phone ______________________

Address _____________________________________ Fax ________________________

____

Will

Date ____________________

Original filed ____

Copies filed____

Letter of Instruction

Date ____________________

Original filed ____

Copies filed____

Executor(s)

Name ____

Address _____________________________________ Phone ______________________

____ Fax ________________________

Name ____

Address _____________________________________ Phone ______________________

____ Fax ________________________

Photographic Advisor

Name ___________________________________ Affiliation _____________________

Address _____________________________________ Phone ______________________

____ Fax ________________________

Additional Advisors/Colleagues to be consulted for photographic advice

Name ___________________________________ Affiliation _____________________

Address _____________________________________ Phone ______________________

____ Fax ________________________

Name ___________________________________ Affiliation _____________________

Address _____________________________________ Phone ______________________

____ Fax ________________________

ESTATE ORGANIZER

TO ____   Date _______________________
               (Executor)

FROM ____
                (Photographer)

ABOUT: Appraising my photographic collection and handling photographic materials

My will makes clear who is to receive my photographs, the copyrights in those photographs and my photographic equipment. The information below is meant as a helpful guide to carrying out my will and handling the appraisal process.

For purposes of appraising the assets in my estate, here is what you need to know about my file. The photographs in my collections have been categorized as follows:

1. Snapshots: These pictures have value as personal memorabilia only and include photographs of family, friends, and assistants. Some were taken on the periphery of an assignment, for fun, others were shot during the course of family life. Any photographs of commercial value have already been placed in the stock file or with my stock agency. They can be held as souvenirs or thrown out. These do not have commercial value.
Location where this material is filed ____

2. Experiments: These pictures relate to film, lighting and other tests and were kept for reference only. Any photographs of commercial value have already been placed in the stock file or with my stock agency. They can be thrown out. These do not have commercial value.
Location where this material is filed ____

3. Samples: these photos were kept as samples of lighting or technical difficulties, models or locations to be used again, or useful props or set decorations. Any photos of value have already been removed. They can be thrown out. These do not have commercial value.
Location where this material is filed ____

4. Rejects: There shouldn't be any, except for recent shoots, but if there are boxes or folders marked "rejects" still around, they can be discarded now. These do not have commercial value.
Location where this material is kept ____

5. Portfolio:
❑ **a.** had value only during my lifetime since it was used to get assignment work and my presence was required. The value of the portfolio ceases when I am not there to perform the assignment. There is no commercial value.
❑ **b.** has no value as stock since the portfolio is comprised of duplicates of originals already on file with my stock agency . There is no commercial value.
❑ **c.** has no value as stock since it consists of tearsheets, prints and laminates which have no reproduction value and were samples used to secure assignments. There is no commercial value.
If none of the above, then (d) applies
❑ **d.** has value as stock and should be offered to my stock agency.
Location where portfolio is usually kept ____

6. Historical:
❑ **a.** These pictures are out of date for current commercial use but may have significance to a museum or historical archive. You may wish to consider donating them and taking any applicable tax savings.
❑ **b.** These pictures are out of date for current commercial use but may have significance to a historical photo agency. You may wish to consider placing them with a historical photo agency. If a historical photo agency declines to accept them, then they have no commercial value.

❑ **c.** These pictures are out of date for current commercial use and probably have little future value. They can be disposed of as the heirs see fit.

❑ **d.** Because of the subject matter and style of my work, any photographs shot before_____________ date or more than _________ years ago can be considered out of date or historical even though they might not have been separated from the main file. They have no commercial value.

Location (if not in main file)____

7. Special collections:

The following are special segments of my work which may be treated differently from the general file:

a. Collection ____

Offer to institution ____

b. Collection ____

Offer to institution ____

Location (if not in main file) ____

8. My stock photo file

a. has continuing income producing value and you may consider having it maintained by _________________________________ (name)

b. has continuing value only if placed with a stock agency. Consult my photo advisor or agency for evaluation and editing of material in my file.

My stock file can be found ____

9. Photos on file with stock agency.

a. When the stock agency contract term is up, use your best judgment with respect to renewal or consult with my photographic advisor.

b. An inventory of photographs currently on file with my stock agency or agencies can be found _________________________________

The Stock Photo Agencies listed below are currently representing my work.

Advise them that future payments should be made to ____
(Name)

Agency Name ____

Contact ____________________________________ Phone ____________________________

Address ____________________________________ Fax ____________________________

____

Agency Name ____

Contact ____________________________________ Phone ____________________________

Address ____________________________________ Fax ____________________________

____

Agency Name ____

Contact ____________________________________ Phone ____________________________

Address ____________________________________ Fax ____________________________

____

Agency Name ____

Contact ____________________________________ Phone ____________________________

Address ____________________________________ Fax ____________________________

____